NWH

P9-EDN-899

j796.72
Mello, Tara Baukus.
The pit crew

OCT 1 5 1998

ALLEN COUNTY PUBLIC LIBRARY
FORT WAYNE, INDIANA 46802

You may return this book to any agency, branch,
or bookmobile of the Allen County Public Library

DEMCO

RACE CAR LEGENDS

CHELSEA HOUSE PUBLISHERS

THE
PIT CREW

Tara Baukus Mello

CHELSEA HOUSE PUBLISHERS
Philadelphia

Allen County Public Library
900 Webster Street
PO Box 2270
Fort Wayne, IN 46801-2270

Frontis: Al Unser's pit crew refuels and re-tires Unser's car at the 1972 Indianapolis 500.

Produced by Type Shoppe II Productions, Ltd.
Chestertown, Maryland

Picture research by Joseph W. Wagner

CHELSEA HOUSE PUBLISHERS

Editor in Chief: Stephen Reginald
Managing Editor: James Gallagher
Production Manager: Pamela Loos
Art Director: Sara Davis
Picture Editor: Judy L. Hasday
Senior Production Editor: Lisa Chippendale
Publishing Coordinator: James McAvoy
Cover Illustration: Keith Trego

Cover Photos: AP/Wide World Photos

Copyright © 1999 by Chelsea House Publishers, a division of Main Line Book Co. All rights reserved. Printed and bound in the United States of America.

First Printing

1 3 5 7 9 8 6 4 2

The Chelsea House Publishers World Wide Web site address is
http://www.chelseahouse.com

Library of Congress Cataloging-in-Publication Data
Mello, Tara Baukus.
    The pit crew / Tara Baukus Mello.
    p.   cm. — (Race car legends)
    Includes bibliographical references and index.
    Summary: Examines the history and importance of the pit crew
in auto racing.
    ISBN 0-7910-5022-X (alk. paper)
    1. Automobile racing—Juvenile literature. 2. Pit crews—
Juvenile literature [1. Automobile racing. 2. Pit crews.] I.
Title. II. Series.
GV1029.M47 1998
796.72—dc21   98–19266
                                                              CIP
                                                               AC

CONTENTS

IN THE PITS

Being in the pit area at a race track is the most exciting place to be in auto racing, unless you are in the driver's seat, of course. Like locker room interviews after the big game, activity in the pits gives fans an up-close look at racing.

The driver is the person who pilots his car to victory, but that would not be possible without the pit crew working to make sure that the car is in perfect condition for the race. In all types of auto racing, the pit crew is made up of a group of people behind the scenes, who are in charge of setting up the car for competition. Each member of the pit crew has a different duty, but the members must work together to prepare the car properly for the race.

Teamwork is critical for any pit crew. In many forms of racing, such as stock car racing, crew members practice their pit stop rou-

A stop on pit row during the 1997 Indianapolis 500. Pit crew team members change tires, refuel the car, check the suspension, and clean the windshield, all with split-second timing.

tines to make sure they work on the car as fast as possible on race day. A pit stop occurs when the driver stops in the pit area during a race to have essential work performed, such as fueling or changing tires. This type of pit stop is performed during many kinds of racing, including drag racing. Even off-road racing has pit stops, but often the pit crew sets up the pit area alongside the race course instead of in a designated area, such as the infield of a race track.

In drag racing, drivers race on a quarter-mile track. Each round of the race lasts only a few seconds. Because each round is so short, drivers don't take pit stops like they do in stock car racing; instead they go to their pit

The pit crew replaces the nose cone of Arie Luyendyk's car after it was damaged in a collision at the 1996 Indy 500.

areas between each round. There, the pit crew makes adjustments to the car to make it go faster in the next round. Sometimes, if there has been a minor accident or a mechanical problem during the round, the pit crew has to perform major work on the car. Some drag racing pit crews have replaced car bodies, and even engines, between rounds. Although there is no way for a drag racing team to practice pit stops as teams do in other types of racing, everyone knows that working quickly means the difference between winning and losing.

Speed is important on the track, and the speed of the pit crew is important off the track. To make things go faster, each crew member has a specific job. For example, in the National Association for Stock Car Automobile Racing (NASCAR) Winston Cup circuit, there is one person who puts fuel in the car. In drag racing, one person packs the parachutes that enable the drivers to stop at the end of the quarter-mile. In off-road racing, one person points the driver to the right pit area, often with a flashlight, because many races last into the evening. Each person on the pit crew is equally important, because without each member doing his or her job, the driver will not be able to do his or her best on the track, and even worse, might crash.

The person who oversees the pit crew is the crew chief. On some race teams, the crew chief works on the car; on other teams, the crew chief acts as supervisor. On all teams, however, the crew chief is the person who makes the decisions about what is done to the race car every time it enters the pit area. Every race depends on two things: a car that

Ferrari pit crew swarm all around their race car at the 1996 Australian Grand Prix in Melbourne. Driver Eddie Irvine took a third place with this car's debut.

is tuned to win, and a driver who can drive that car to the finish line first. No matter how good the driver is, he or she will not be able to win unless the car is tuned correctly. As a result, the crew chief must make the right decisions.

The crew chief relies on information and people to help. The crew chief talks to the driver about how the car performed while it was on the track; analyzes data from computers that show what was happening to the car during each turn; takes into consideration the weather, altitude, and condition of the track; and puts all of these factors together to

3 1822 02202 6575

make decisions about how to improve the car's performance.

Experience is the key to making the right decisions. The longer the crew chief has worked around race cars, and the longer he has been with the team, the more likely he is to make decisions that help the driver win the race. That is why no one starts out as a crew chief. Crew chiefs have to work their way up through the ranks before they get the top position.

Today, big-name sponsors and increased money winnings have made auto racing a highly technical sport. As a result, crew chiefs often spend more time looking at computer screens than they do looking under the hoods of race cars. For example, Ray Evernham, crew chief for NASCAR Winston Cup champion Jeff Gordon, said, "I've had to spend a lot

Pit crew behind the wall, waiting for their car to come in for a quick tire change and fuel at the Brickyard 400.

An Indianapolis 500–style race car in pit row gets fuel via two hoses and has worn tires replaced.

of time reading up on things I should have paid attention to in high school."

Understanding the technology behind racing could be the key to getting a job with a pit crew in the future. Teams now are hiring engineers and computer specialists to give them the competitive edge they need to win. Some experts speculate that in the future, a college degree might be a requirement to become a member of the pit crew of a top team.

Crew members' salaries vary greatly. The most junior members of the team, those with the least experience, are paid the lowest. Members with the most experience receive higher salaries. In NASCAR Winston Cup racing, for example, a crew chief can make as little as $75,000 or as much as $400,000, depending on the person's experience and the success of the team.

Pit crews are generally on the road more than they are at home. In many types of auto racing, there is a race nearly every weekend during the season. Days, both at the track and at the team shop, are often long, and crew members sometimes work until 3 A.M. only to report to work again at 8 A.M. the next morning. Because the stakes are high, everyone feels the pressure to win, but the bottom line for every member of the pit crew in every type of auto racing is that they love racing. They are willing to spend long hours at work, endless days on the road, and time away from their families in exchange for the feeling they get when they see their team car cross the finish line first.

STOCK CAR RACING

NASCAR is the fastest growing sport in America today. In 1997, about 8.3 million people watched the Daytona 500 on television. Sponsors sell or give away thousands of items promoting their drivers every year. And the most popular drivers hand out about 300,000 driver cards to fans each year at the races.

In stock car racing, there are seven crew members that "go over the wall", or over the barrier that separates the pit crews from the cars as they pull into pit lane. Together, the pit crew performs its duties in a well-practiced performance. It is not uncommon for a Winston Cup pit crew to practice their pit stops once a week, or even more often.

The crew chief decides when the driver should come into the pits. This decision is based on many things, such as how much fuel the car has left, if the tires need changing,

The pit crew of race car driver Dale Jarrett celebrates after he won the 1998 TransSouth Financial 400 at Darlington Raceway, South Carolina.

how well the car is handling as decided by the track conditions, and if the race is currently under a yellow caution flag, which means that drivers must hold their positions and not pass other cars. Each team has a stall on pit row. When the driver reaches the pit stall before his, his pit crew is allowed to jump over the wall. Once the car has stopped, the jackman, front and rear tire changers, and front and rear tire carriers run around to the passenger side of the car. While the jackman raises the car off the ground, the two tire changers loosen the

Gasman and catch-can man fueling a Winston Cup car. Top pit crew teams can complete a pit stop in 20 seconds or less.

lug nuts. Once the tire is off, the tire carriers hand a new tire to the changers who put it on and tighten the lugs. The process is then repeated on the opposite side of the car.

At the same time, a gasman and a catch-can man refuel the car. The gasman fills the fuel tank using a can that contains 11 gallons of racing gas and which weighs about 80 pounds. The catch-can man's job is to hold a can at the opening of a small vent in the rear of the car to catch any excess fuel. The fuel is then weighed to determine exactly how much fuel was put into the car.

While these seven people are hard at work, several people assist them from behind the wall. Each tire carrier has an assistant who hands a fresh tire over the wall. A second gasman hands a second can of fuel over the wall to the first gasman, who puts it in the car. Another person washes the windshield using a squeegee mounted on a long pole. Someone gives the driver a drink by passing it to him on another long pole. When the jackman drops the car for the second time, the driver heads back out onto the track.

Today, the top teams complete a pit stop in less than 20 seconds. But in the beginning of stock car racing, it wasn't unusual for teams to take a minute or more during a pit stop. Often, if the team had to pit when the rest of the cars were racing, they lost an entire lap during the pit stop. Winston Cup racing was more than 10 years old when a team first realized that they could gain an advantage if they could shorten their pit stops.

In 1960, Wood Brothers Racing discovered that they could cut some pit stops in half with a bit of effort. At that time, a pit stop where two tires were changed and the car was refueled lasted about 48 seconds. By practicing pit stops and deciding where each crew member would be, Wood Brothers reduced the time for this type of pit stop to 23 seconds.

Pit stops also took longer in the 1960s and 1970s because of the equipment that was used. Back then, a jack weighed 80 pounds and took many pumps to raise the car high enough to change the tires. In addition, tire changers used four-prong wrenches instead of high-speed air guns to loosen and tighten the lug nuts. And extra time was spent tightening the gas cap, which the gasman used to have to screw on and off manually.

Earlier stock car racing took place in cow pastures and at the beach. In addition, there weren't any rules: anybody could race against anybody else, driving any type of car they wanted. The sport quickly became popular, and before long, people paid to come to watch the races. The drivers split the money raised from the spectators, the majority of which went to the winner. It didn't take long for stock car racing to become competitive, and soon drivers began to add new parts to their cars to make their engines go faster.

In 1934, Bill France visited Daytona Beach, Florida, and was fascinated by the stock car races that were held on the beach. Bill found it so exciting that he moved to Florida so he, too, could race. In December of 1947 he held a meeting with other drivers in the area, and they formed NASCAR. The first NASCAR race was held in February of 1948. Half the track was on the sand of Daytona Beach and the other half on the street that ran alongside the beach. This race became the Daytona 500 that is shown on national television today.

Also in the early days of stock car racing, communication between the driver and his crew, once he was on the track, was minimal. Teams gathered together before the race to decide the strategy, and the only time they could talk was during a pit stop. Because this was not very effective, crew members began to use large chalkboards to relay messages to the drivers. Pit crews would write messages on the chalkboard and hold it up as the drivers raced

An early Daytona 500 stock car race and pit area before present-day sophisticated methods were developed.

by their pit stalls. Unfortunately, the message board wasn't very effective either. Reading the board meant that drivers had to take their eyes off the race track to glance over at the pits and read the sign. In addition, drivers could only respond after they had passed the pits, read the sign, and completed another lap.

To help improve this situation a system of hand signals was created so drivers could send messages to pit crews. If they needed tires for the right side of the car, for example, they would put two fingers on the roof as they passed the pit stall; if they needed two tires for the left side, they would put two fingers on the door. If the car was overheating, the drivers would hold their noses.

Although this was more effective, communication really wasn't much improved until two-way radios were invented. Today, radios smaller than videotapes that plug into the drivers' helmets are used. To talk to pit crews, drivers push a button on the steering wheel and talk into microphones mounted in their helmets. When the pit crew responds, drivers usually hear them clearly through an earpiece, also mounted in the helmet, which has been custom-fitted for their ears.

The person that usually talks to the driver during the race is the crew chief. Todd Parrott is crew chief for the Dale Jarrett Ford Quality Care/Ford Credit racing team. In 1996, his first year with this sponsor, Dale was the first driver ever to win the Daytona 500 and the Brickyard 400 in the same year, and finished third in the championship behind Terry Labonte and Jeff Gordon. Todd, who spent 17 years as a crew member, took on his first crew-chief position with this team at the end of 1995. From the start, Dale and Todd were great together, and won the first two events of the year, the Busch Clash and the Daytona 500.

As crew chief, Todd manages the 15 to 20 people that make up the crew for Dale's car. As happens on many teams, the crew members of the Quality Care/Ford Credit team wear many hats. Often, crew members have one job at the races and a different job at the race shop. Tommy Mullis and Jason Burdett

Pit crew members work on Dale Jarrett's car in his last pit stop before winning the UAW-GM Quality 500 at the Charlotte Motor Speedway. Jarrett beat Bobby Labonte out of the pits and led the rest of the way.

are good examples of crew members that have several different jobs on Dale's crew.

Tommy Mullis's main job is to drive the truck and trailer from the shop to the races and back home again. Tommy drives about 60,000 miles each year, usually to or from races, at least three days a week during race season. As part of his job, Tommy unloads everything in preparation for the race. Once the race is completed he reloads all the equipment and replenishes the parts that have been used. Although this job sounds simple, it is critical: the team must know exactly where the parts they need are located, and they must be able to count on the fact that Tommy has replaced used parts with new ones. When the team is at the track, Tommy becomes the

Dale Jarrett of Newton, North Carolina, has an early pit stop in the 1997 Brickyard 400 at the Indianapolis Motor Speedway. Teammate Ernie Irvan goes by to his pit area.

catch-can man. Every time Dale comes into the pits, Tommy jumps over the wall and holds the can at the special vent while the gasman fuels the car. The fuel caught in the can is weighed so the team can calculate exactly how much fuel went into Dale's car and how many miles he can travel.

The newest member of Dale's team is also the youngest. Tire specialist Jason Burdett started on the team in 1997 when he was just 19 years old. Jason is a mechanic at the shop, and does basic preparation work, such as cleaning filters and repacking engine bearings. At the track, Jason is responsible for the tires. Robert Yates Racing, the team owner, takes tires very seriously, and it is up to Jason to make sure everything is right.

Goodyear supplies all the race teams with tires before each race. Jason picks up the team's tires, often 12 sets, and looks at the code numbers and letters on the sidewalls. Using the code, he matches the tires up in sets of four as closely as possible to get tires that will perform well together.

Once Dale is out on the track, Jason checks the air pressure of the tires. Jason gives the air pressure readings to Todd, who decides how to adjust them to best handle the condition of the track. Jason adjusts air pressure about 100 times during a race.

Few people will ever have the opportunity to join the crew of a Winston Cup team. For those given the opportunity, it is a dream come true. For Todd, Tommy, and Jason, they know that what they do means the difference between winning and losing.

3

DRAG RACING

Blink your eyes. In the time that it took you to blink, a Top Fuel dragster covered the length of a football field.

Speed is what makes all types of auto racing exciting. Whether the racers are on dirt or asphalt, or racing in a circle, on the street, or in a straight line, it is the roar of the engine as the car zooms by that causes your heart to skip a beat. Of all the types of racing, drag racing is the fastest. Professional drag racers can go over 300 miles per hour (mph) in the quarter-mile race, which means that the entire race lasts for about four seconds.

In drag races, two cars race side-by-side on a track that is a quarter of a mile long. Racers are matched in pairs and race against each other. The driver with the faster time progresses to the next round of competition and the slower is eliminated. When there are only two competitors left, the racer with the faster time wins the competition.

An early drag racer, amidst tire smoke, roars down a track lined with spectators.

There are three professional classes in drag racing: Top Fuel, Funny Car, and Pro Stock. Top Fuel is the fastest class, where racers drive rear-engine dragsters. Funny Cars, which make up the next fastest class, are basically front-engine dragsters with fiberglass bodies that resemble passenger cars, such as the Ford Mustang or Pontiac Trans-Am, although they are shorter and have long noses and fat tails. The term Funny Car goes back to the 1960s when drag racers took stock cars and moved the rear wheels forward, raised the nose, and made other changes that made the car look funny. People referred to them as Funny Cars, and the name stuck. Funny Cars have a supercharger that sticks up through the hood, and the driver sits where the rear

John Force, three-time defending Funny Car champion, competes in the finals with a run for the quarter-mile at 285.17 mph.

seat used to be. Funny Cars don't have doors. Instead, the body must be lifted up at the front in order for the driver to enter. Pro Stock is a class of racing cars that most closely resembles today's street cars. Pro Stock cars are usually Fords or Chevys, and are the exact length and width of the cars after which they are modeled. Instead of being made of steel, certain parts, such as the hood, front fenders, and rear deck, are replaced with lightweight versions, often made of fiberglass.

Before a drag race, the crew drives a truck or a van that tows the car to the starting line. When the driver's turn comes, the engine is started and the driver does a "burnout," or spins the rear wheels of the car. When this happens, smoke billows off the tires. This heats the rubber on the tires and gives the car traction as it heads down the track. The rear tires are made of a special rubber that is soft and gummy and allows them to grip the track.

After the burnout, the driver makes a practice run part way down the track. This practice run is called a "dry-hop," and heats up the clutch in preparation for the race. The driver then has to drive backward to the starting line. It is important that the car is straight at the starting line, so a crew member stands in front of the car and directs the driver while he or she backs up. Once the driver backs up all the way, the crew member directs the driver to pull forward to the starting line, where there is an electronic beam that activates a timer when the driver leaves the line. At the end of the quarter-mile, the electronic beam stops the timer and instantly flashes the elapsed time and the speed of each vehicle onto a large screen for the spectators to see.

Once the drivers are in position, a race official called a starter activates the "Christmas tree." The Christmas tree is an electronically controlled system of red, yellow, and green lights mounted on a tall pole between the two lanes just past the starting line. At the top of the pole, two yellow lights flash a signal to the driver that his or her car is near the starting line. A second set of yellow lights come on when the car is ready for its run. These are called the "staging lights." Once the cars are staged, five yellow countdown lights go on from top to bottom. Four-tenths of a second after the last yellow light comes on, the green light flashes. The green light is the drivers signal to go. If the driver leaves the starting line before the green light, the red light comes on and the driver is disqualified from the race.

Drag racing wasn't always this sophisticated. In the beginning, there was simply a flagman and a person who timed the race with a stopwatch. The first drag races were run on dry lake beds in the 1930s. Racers drove their Model T and Model A Fords to the race course and stripped off certain parts, such as fenders, windshields, and lights to make the car more aerodynamic. When the race was over, the drivers replaced the parts on their cars and drove home.

In 1937, a group called the Southern California Timing Association (SCTA) was formed, and drag racing, called hot rodding, got more serious. The SCTA made decisions about ambulance service in case of an accident, and created a points system to determine who would be the champion of a series of races.

In 1949, the president of the SCTA, Wally Parks, became the editor of a new magazine called *Hot Rod*. One day, a reader wrote to Wally and asked why there wasn't a national organization devoted to hot rodding. Wally and the magazine publishers liked the idea and the National Hot Rod Association (NHRA) was formed with Wally as president. As of 1998, Wally is still president. In 1953, the first city-sponsored, NHRA-organized race was held in Pomona, California. Today, the first and last races of the NHRA season are held at the

In 1998 Kenny Bernstein set a track record of 320.74 mph at the Pomona Raceway, Pomona, California.

Blaine Johnson, drag chutes deployed, finishes one of his qualifying runs at the NHRA Mac Tools Gaternationals held at the Gainesville Raceway, Florida.

Pomona track. Although there are other drag racing organizations, the NHRA is the biggest.

Since race classes rotate throughout the day, spectators can spend the entire day watching races from the grandstands. But many fans, once they have seen their favorite team or race class, often go to the pit area to get an up-close view of their teams in action. Typically, a race team has 90 minutes between passes, or rounds, before they have to race again. During this time, the pits are a flurry of activity as teams prepare the cars for the next race. Unlike other forms of racing, in drag racing fans are allowed in the pit area and can watch their favorite team at work.

Many times, the drivers sign autographs while their team works on the car.

One of the most popular drivers is John Force. A seven-time national champion, John is probably the most entertaining driver in racing today. John races a Funny Car and he is always cracking jokes and telling stories.

One of John's three crew chiefs is Bernie Fedderly. He has been on the team since 1992, but has been involved in racing for a long time. As a crew chief, Bernie handles the mechanical and administrative aspects of running the team.

When the team isn't racing, Bernie is in the Yorba Linda, California, office by 8:30 A.M. If John is not traveling that day, he heads a meeting to update the crew on current activities. Once the meeting is over, Bernie works with Austin Coil and John Medlen, the other two crew chiefs, to discuss the team's strategy or new projects. During the winter, days are especially long, because all the equipment is at the shop being rebuilt. It is not unusual for the crew to work 10 hours a day during this time.

Traveling to the races is a big production for the Force team. In 1998, the team ran two Funny Cars, one driven by John and the other by Tony Pedregon. Since they were racing two cars instead of one, it took 12 people to get all the support vehicles and race equipment to every race. Three big rigs, two support vehicles, and a bus travel to each race.

The Funny Cars each have five crew members assigned to them, plus a crew chief and a driver. Austin Coil works primarily on John's car, whereas John Medlen works mainly on Tony's car. Bernie floats between the two, but works mainly on John's car.

These dragsters mark the early and late stages of Don "The Snake" Prudhomme's drag racing career. At right is the Skoal Bandit raced in 1994, and next to it is a fuel dragster raced in 1964 with over 200 wins to its credit.

Pit stops aren't as fast as they are in other forms of racing, because the crew has a lot of work on the cars between rounds. In just 90 minutes, the team jacks up the car, drains the oil, and downloads the information from the on-board computer. The crew chief analyzes the computer data and decides on a strategy for the next round. Meanwhile, the crew inspects and services most of the parts on the engine, including the supercharger, valves and springs, cylinder heads, engine bearings, and crankshaft. They replace the rods and pistons and reassemble the engine. New sparkplugs, oil, and an oil filter are added. Once the en-

gine work is complete, the engine is started, and the crew makes adjustments and checks it for leaks.

If the car is damaged during one of the rounds, things become hectic for the pit crew. The team always has spare engine parts in their trailer, as well as an extra body for each car. Assuming the driver isn't hurt, the team must be prepared for any problem because if the car is not able to advance to the next round of competition, the team's chances at the championship are in question.

The most difficult problem a pit crew faces is if the car catches on fire during a run. Although many times damage from a fire will put a team out of the race, if the team is well-prepared, they are able to repair the car and continue to race. In cases of fire, the crew must also change most of the rubber hoses because they are often damaged by heat. There are many hoses on these vehicles, and replacing them is a long and tedious job.

At the Mid-South Nationals in Memphis, Tennessee, in 1992, John had a bad accident during the semifinal round of competition and his car caught on fire. Because of this accident, the team felt it was necessary to make safety improvements to protect Funny Car drivers. The team was instrumental in developing a fire shield, a piece on the cowl that protects the driver from the engine during a fire, as well as a fresh air system that helps the driver breathe. Both of these features are used widely by Funny Car racers today.

Being a member of a winning team is fun, but it is also very demanding. During the race season, Force's crew is on the road more than

Don Garlits powers his Top Fuel dragster to a record-setting speed of 268.01 mph at the 1985 World Championships in Pomona, California.

they are at home. Crew members alternate coming home and sometimes bring their families to the track with them during race weekends. Bernie has a slightly better schedule because as crew chief, he usually flies to the races instead of driving like most of the crew. Still, Bernie usually flies out on a Wednesday and doesn't return until the following Sunday or Monday evening. That's about 150 days of travel every year.

Although the schedule is grueling, many people still want to get one of the coveted spots on the team. Bernie admits that getting a position on a race team is pretty difficult for someone new to racing. In general, team owners look for people who have a special skill, such as computer training, truck driving, machining, or fabrication. To Bernie, hiring a new employee who has a college degree is important, but not nearly as important as real-world technical experience. He says the best way to get experience is to participate in the amateur, or Sportsman, classes of racing.

ENDURANCE
RACING

Auto racing is filled with rules. Most racing, however, didn't start out that way. A group of people who loved to drive fast got together to race in a variety of places, from the cow pastures of early Winston Cup racing to the dry lake beds of early drag racing. Now, races are organized by governing bodies, such as NASCAR or NHRA, and have many race officials who oversee every race.

While many officials have many different duties, all officials have one main goal: to make sure that racing is safe. The organizations' rules serve to protect the drivers, crew, and spectators from accidents on the track. Another goal of so many rules is to keep racing fair, so that everyone has an equal chance to win.

Endurance racing has the most rules of all types of racing. In endurance racing, a race team runs one car for 12 or 24 hours straight,

The #3 Scandia Ferrari leaving the pit area after service. Ferrari competed in the January 1998 Rolex 24-hour endurance race in Daytona, Florida.

stopping only to switch drivers, refuel, or repair the car. This type of racing is hard on the race car and on the drivers.

Endurance racing is an international sport, and teams from all over the world travel to many different countries to compete in these long races. Among famous endurance races are the "12 Hours of Sebring," "24 Hours of Daytona," and "24 Hours of Le Mans." Each race is run on a road course, which includes left and right turns and straightaways. Sometimes these races are run on public roads that have been blocked off to regular traffic during the race. At times, endurance races are run on race tracks designed especially for road racing. These tracks are used for other road racing events in addition to endurance races. In endurance racing, the winning team is the one who has driven the most miles at the end of the 12- or 24-hour time period.

One reason why endurance racing seems to have more rules than other types of racing is because there are several different organizations that oversee different races. Each organization has different rules, and teams have to abide by these different rules at every race.

One racing organization that oversees endurance racing is the Sports Car Club of America (SCCA). In the 1940s, a group of people who preferred the European style of road racing founded the SCCA. In the beginning, the racers ran their cars on closed roads and airport runways. Most of the competitors drove sports cars from Europe because they didn't trust American-made cars. The SCCA was also one of the few organizations that allowed women to race.

The start of the 1966 Le Mans 24-hour race in France. Drivers run to
their cars, start their engines, and drive for 24 hours. Each car has a team
of three drivers who alternate.

The first major SCCA race was organized in 1948 at Watkins Glen, New York. Although there is a track there now, this race was held on the town's streets. It was won by Frank Griswold, who drove a pre-World War II Alfa Romeo to victory.

In the early days, anyone could race a car as long as they had the money. Doctors, lawyers, and engineers all raced on weekends when they weren't working at their regular jobs. There was even a showroom class where a person could race the car he or she just purchased at a car dealership without changing anything.

In 1962, many European drivers, and a few Americans, including Mario Andretti, Dan

The Mazda co-driven by Johnny Herbert of Britain, Volker Weidle of Germany, and Bertrand Gachot of Belgium takes the lead at the 1991 24-hour Le Mans endurance race, the first Japanese car ever to win the race.

Gurney, and A. J. Foyt, became well known for this type of racing. Soon, the SCCA formed a professional class for these drivers. Although the SCCA allowed women to race, racing officials didn't like the idea of women racing in the long endurance races. But in 1967, four teams of women raced in the 12 Hours of Sebring.

The Sebring track is located in central Florida a few miles north of Lake Okeechobee, and was originally a military base for B-17 bomber training. The maze of airplane runways and service roads was converted into a race course that has been called an American version of the 24 Hours of Le Mans. The course is 5.2 miles of pretzel-shaped twists and turns that are known to cause many mechanical problems for the race cars. Drivers frequently race down the straightaways at over 150 miles per hour at Sebring, only to be forced to slow down to enter hairpin curves. Slowing down quickly is not easy. The drivers must double downshift through the gears, while stomping on the brakes. The car skids and sways under the strain as the tires squeal in an effort to stop. All this strain means that the car could break apart at any time and have to pull into the pits for repair.

One team that competes in road racing, including 12-and 24-hour endurance races, is the Saleen/Allen "RRR" Speedlab. The team was formed in 1995 as a partnership between Steve Saleen, race car driver and owner of Saleen Performance, a specialty vehicle manufacturer, and *Home Improvement* television star Tim Allen. The name "RRR" comes from Tim's television character Tim "Tool Man"

Taylor's grunting noise. Tim owns a souped-up Saleen Mustang. While the company was building it, Steve and Tim became friends. Before long, they started a race team in which both Tim and Steve, among others, were the drivers.

The team races Saleen Mustang SRs that have over 500 horsepower. In 1996, just one year after the team was founded, they won the SCCA World Challenge Sports class series.

Crew chief Dave Walsh has been with the team since 1995. It is his responsibility to oversee all aspects of the race team. When Steve and Tim made the decision to start their own race team, they only had seven weeks to prepare for their first race. Dave was part of the small, core group of four people that built the cars and prepped the transporter for that first race.

The team keeps Dave busy even when they are off the track and at the shop. At any time, Dave oversees at least eight crew members, and sometimes more if they are running two cars in a season. He assigns each crew member a list of duties, and supervises all of the preparations. In addition, he makes sure that certain parts are tested for wear, double checks the quality of parts as they come in, and supervises the bodywork and engine rebuilds that are done to the race car.

A substantial portion of Dave's job also involves record keeping. He checks over the stock of parts in the trailer, maintains the mileage log for parts that are in use so he knows how much wear they have, schedules parts to be sent out for repairs, and handles the purchase of new parts.

Dave and the Speedlab crew had a busy

year in 1997. Instead of trying to win the championship two years in a row, the team went on a "world tour," and raced in some of the most famous races, including the 24 Hours of Le Mans. Competing in this race was important, not only because it is the most famous of all endurance races, but also because it was the first time that a Mustang had been raced at Le Mans since a Shelby Mustang was raced there in 1967.

The 24 Hours of Le Mans also is considered the most demanding of all the endurance races. It is comprised of just over eight miles of public roads with tunnels, dips, and bridges in addition to its famous twists and turns.

The town of Le Mans is located 130 miles southwest of Paris, France, and is filled with textile factories. Every year in June, the town roars to life with some of the most spectacular cars in the world which gather there to compete in the thrilling but grueling race.

One of the keys to winning any type of race is to have a well-built car that doesn't break down on the track. Although this is important to any team, it is especially important to those competing in endurance races. The crew must be sure that each part is of the highest quality so it can survive the strain of being used for 12 or 24 hours straight. For example, during the 24 Hours of Le Mans, the average winning car travels over 3,000 miles—the distance from New York City to Los Angeles—or even further.

Having a strategy for pit stops is absolutely essential. The Saleen/Allen team usually comes into the pits every hour. At that time, they often switch drivers, although occasionally, a driver takes a double shift of two hours

A typical endurance racer rounding a turn at the 1969 24 Hours of Le Mans race.

at the wheel. The car is refueled and jacked up into the air. The wheels come off, and the brakes and other components are inspected. If everything looks good, the driver heads back out onto the track. But if something isn't right, the crew has to be prepared to fix whatever is wrong.

Unfortunately, there are many things that can go wrong and parts that need to be replaced because they've simply worn out. On the Saleen/Allen team, the chief engineer decides what adjustments to make on the car, including when to switch drivers and when to refuel. The goal is for the driver to take it easy with the car overall. In endurance racing, being conservative is what wins. If the driver always has the gas pedal to the floor, he's more likely to break something on the car. That means longer pit stops, or worse, getting knocked out of the race.

Typically, the Saleen/Allen team will need to replace a portion of the brakes—the rotors, the pads, or both—about every four hours. The team has an advantage over European cars because Mustangs are economical with fuel: since they don't need to refuel as often, they can go longer between pit stops. That is, if nothing else goes wrong with the car. At the 1997 24 Hours of Le Mans, the team had to replace the gearbox three times because the drivers had to switch gears so often they kept damaging it.

Pit stops at Le Mans have more rules than other endurance races. In fact, compared to the lightning fast stops in Winston Cup or Indy Car racing, these pit stops seem to be in slow motion. When the car first comes into the

The start of the 1996 24-hour Le Mans endurance race. The Porsche GT driven by Yannick Dalmas takes the lead, and the Ferrari driven by Didier Theys is in second place. Forty-eight cars took the start in the 64th running of the race.

pits, the driver is required to stop the car completely and shut off the engine before any work can begin. While the car is being refueled, no one else is allowed to work on the car. After refueling, four mechanics can begin their work. For the Saleen/Allen team, a quick pit stop (where there are only basic changes) is about one and a half minutes. If a major part of the car breaks down, it is not uncommon for endurance racing teams to spend an hour or more in the pits.

Each crew member wears a colored vest to designate his role during the pit stop. The scorers wear blue, the crew chief wears red, and the suppliers wear green armbands. A marshal is assigned to each pit. It is his job to make sure that everyone obeys the rules. Anyone who does not receives a penalty.

Racing at Le Mans is very expensive. It costs over one million dollars for the Saleen/Allen team to compete in this one race. The prize money isn't as large an amount as for some other races, but the team felt it was important to compete and show that Mustangs could make their mark. Being accepted into the field by other, more seasoned, manufacturers wasn't easy. At first, the other teams didn't think they were very good, But once the team went into qualifying races and showed their car's capabilities, the others began to pay attention. In fact, everyone was talking about the Saleen Mustangs when the 24 Hours of Le Mans began on Saturday, June 14, 1997. Although both cars qualified, neither one finished the race. The first of the two cars went out after 28 laps because its electrical system failed. The second car completed 133 laps before it had suspension problems and had to leave the race. All in all, only 17 cars out of the 48 that started finished the 24-hour race.

OFF-ROAD RACING

Auto racing is incredibly tough on a driver's body. Every race car driver must be in good physical condition to meet the demands of tremendous g-forces greater than the highest roller-coaster ride, and blazing heat that comes from the engine of a car that's been running for hours. Racing is a test of stamina of both driver and vehicle, and stamina is what wins races.

As the name indicates, off-road races are run off the road. The courses are mapped out by race organizers and are marked with flags. Every car that participates in an off-road race carries two people: a driver and a navigator. The navigator makes sure that the car stays on the course by using the course map and watching out for the course markers.

Some teams have a Global Positioning System (GPS) to ensure that they don't get

Bill Stroppe, master off-road racer builder and navigator, sits at the wheel of a Bronco similar to the one he and Parnelli Jones used to win overall and class championships in the 1973 Baja 500.

lost. A GPS is a small computer that tells the team where they are. The GPS sends a signal to a satellite, which determines where the signal is coming from, then sends the information back to the GPS. The information is translated into longitude and latitude coordinates. By using the coordinates, the navigator can pinpoint the car's exact location by using a map with longitude and latitude lines. Because Global Positioning Systems are fairly new and very expensive, many teams aren't fortunate enough to have them.

An off-road race course covers many different types of terrain, such as dirt roads, dry riverbeds, tidal pools near beaches, rocks, canyons, and even mountains trails. Because of the different types of terrain, off-road racers drive at many different speeds. A driver may travel at only 20 miles per hour through a very difficult section, then speed up to 140 miles per hour when the course becomes less dangerous. Good navigation is important because sometimes the course can be especially treacherous in some places. In fact, some off-road racers have been known to drive off cliffs because they couldn't see where they were going.

Racing on all that uneven ground is very hard on the driver and the navigator. Half of the time inside the race vehicle is spent going forward; the other half is spent going up and down. And the noise is incredible. Every component on the vehicle groans and screams under the pressure. Things rattle and shake and it is nearly impossible to hear anything or anyone.

The oldest and most famous of all off-road

races is the Tecate SCORE Baja 1000. The Baja 1000 takes place in November, and begins in Ensenada, Baja California, Mexico. Usually, the Baja 1000 starts in Ensenada, makes a giant loop through Baja California, and ends back in Ensenada where it began.

Rod Hall, a veteran Baja 1000 racer who has been victorious in his class a record 15 times, with one of his winning vehicles.

Depending on how the race organizers lay it out, the course ranges from 700 to over 1000 miles.

Many years ago, when the race first started, the course started in Ensenada and finished in La Paz, close to the end of the Baja California peninsula. Today, the race organizers skip the loop race every three or four years, and the race is held from Ensenada to La Paz instead. When organizers use the straight route from Ensenada to La Paz, it costs more than twice as much as the loop course. Race teams can expect to spend double the amount of money when running the straight course. Because amateurs and professionals race in the Baja 1000, using the straight route every year would mean not as many teams could afford to participate.

In the year 2000, the race organizers will run the Baja 2000, from Ensenada to La Paz and back. It is sure to be the most demanding off-road race ever run, and will likely draw amateur and professional racers from all around the world.

The first known record run was in 1962 when Dave Elkins and Bill Robertson Jr. timed their trip from Tijuana to La Paz on a pair of Honda 250 motorcycles. It took Dave Elkins 39 hours and 54 minutes, while his partner took less than an hour longer. There were no official rules because it wasn't a real race. To prove that they had completed their run in the time they said, the two went to the telegraph office in Tijuana and time-stamped a sheet of paper. When they arrived in La Paz, they had the same sheet time-stamped at the telegraph office there.

Chevrolet heard about the motorcycle rac-ers' efforts. They hired a legendary car builder named Bill Stroppe to build a fleet of trucks to do the same thing. When all of the trucks made it to La Paz, advertising and publicity campaigns called their feat "the toughest run under the sun."

Before long the National Off-Road Racing Association (NORRA) was formed, and the Mexican 1000 was born in 1967. The Mexican 1000 eventually became known as the Baja 1000. From 1967 to 1973, the Baja 1000 was run from Ensenada to La Paz every year but

Rod Hall arriving at dusk at one of many pit areas for the Baja 1000.

1972, when it was started in Mexicali. In 1973, Mexican officials revoked NORRA's privileges to stage races in Baja. And the 1974 race was cancelled because of the gas crisis. But that wasn't the end of the Baja 1000.

After the fuel crisis was over, the northern state of Baja California invited a group, SCORE International, to hold the race in 1975. SCORE mapped out the loop route that begins and ends in Ensenada, and has organized the race ever since. Today SCORE can use whichever route they choose to run the race. In 1997 the Baja 1000 was run on the loop course beginning and ending in Ensenada. It was 707.7 miles long. There were

Rod Hall's sons, Chad and Josh, are both following in their father's footsteps. Here they race the Hummer in the Baja 500.

approximately 250,000 fans that viewed the race from various checkpoints along the race course, as well as from the start/finish line.

One vehicle leaves the start line every 30 seconds as the fans cheer it on. The teams blast off down the canyon, the noises of their engines revving at full speed echoing off the walls. Some of the more powerful vehicles spray gravel onto the hoods of cars parked as far away as two blocks. And they're off, for 14 hours and more, on the most demanding race in the world.

The driver and navigator are alone much of the time during the race. Chase trucks follow the race vehicles using less demanding roads. The race car stays in radio contact with the chase trucks and pit crews. Every few miles, the navigator radios in their position so the crew can keep track of the vehicle. Many times during the course, the race vehicle is out of radio range, such as when it is traveling through a canyon, so it is important that the crew know where the race vehicle is as often as possible. If the vehicle breaks down, the crew must be able to find them quickly so only a little of the precious race time is lost.

Rod Hall is a veteran Baja 1000 racer. He has competed in every race since the first one in 1967. Rod, who was 59 years old in 1997, is the only person who raced in the first Baja 1000 and is still racing today. Rod has been victorious in his class a record 15 times and, in 1969, was the first one to cross the finish line out of all the classes.

Rod's two sons, Chad and Josh, also race and are involved in the family business, Rod Hall International. The Halls teach off-road and high-performance driving when they are not racing. They race Hummers, which take a team of two people working full-time for 30 days to prepare for the off-road racing event.

When preparing for a race, Hall's crew checks over every component of the vehicle. Because teams aren't allowed to reinforce the stock vehicles, many items have to be replaced after a race. Suspension components, such as crossmembers and a-arms, are inspected for cracks and other wear. The crew takes nearly the entire vehicle apart and inspects every piece carefully. Sometimes items are replaced, other times, the same part is reinstalled. The Halls' Hummers have an engine and transmission which almost duplicate the ones that come from the factory, but they use hand-made tires that are much sturdier than the tires used on passenger vehicles.

Sometimes during a race, a part breaks down on the vehicle and the team is too far away from the pit crew. In these instances the driver and navigator have to fix the car by themselves. The Hummer carries many spare parts in case of such an emergency. The crew stocks the vehicle with parts that are needed in order for the car to move, but which aren't big or heavy. Parts carried include ball joints, fuses, electrical wire, a fan belt, and spare tires. It is the race teams who have the best prepared vehicles that win the race, not the ones who go the fastest.

To prepare for the Baja 1000, the drivers have the opportunity to make a trial run on the course. This enables them to learn the route and look for dangerous areas, such as big holes. They use a special computer to note certain landmarks and dangerous spots along the course. During the race, this computer helps guide them. The trial run allows the drivers to determine where their chase vehicles should be placed. The Halls have five or six support vehicles stationed at various places along the course to help them if their car breaks down.

During the race, there are pit stops about every 120 miles. Since the crew can't see where the team car is on the course, the driver

Typical pit stop area during the Baja 500 or 1000, where drivers pick up fuel and tires and make repairs.

radios ahead to tell the crew how far away he is from the pit area so the crew can get ready for his arrival. When the vehicle enters the pits, a crew member dumps 40 gallons of fuel into the car while other members of the team check the tires. The pit crew checks under the hood and under the vehicle, looking for any areas that are wet. Because it is dry and dusty in the desert, wet spots usually mean there is a leak somewhere.

More often than not, something will go wrong with the vehicle when the driver is nowhere near the pit area. It has happened many times to the Halls. In the 1997 Baja 1000, Chad was driving when the steering column began to come apart. The rivets that held the mounting bracket together came loose, and the steering column was moving up and

Every pit stop area has a collection of fuel cans, tires, and necessary spare parts for repairs.

down about four inches. Chad knew he would have to stop and fix it quickly. He took vice grips and motorcycle straps out of the tool kit. He used the vice grips to hold the column in place, and then looped the straps over the roll bar to make sure the column wouldn't move when he started to drive again. He had the problem solved in about five minutes.

In order to win, or even to finish a Baja 1000 race, the driver must know not to push himself or the vehicle too far. Rod Hall says that knowing his vehicle's ability, and being a disciplined driver, are what got him into the winner's circle so many times. The Baja 1000 is a much more intense race today than it was when it first started. But the most important thing is reaching the finish line, because just finishing one of the toughest races in the world is certainly an accomplishment.

CHRONOLOGY

1934   Bill France visits Daytona Beach, Florida, and is fascinated by the stock car racing he sees on the beach.

1947   The National Association for Stock Car Automobile Racing (NASCAR) is formed.

1948   The first NASCAR race is held in Daytona Beach, Florida.

1932   The first drag races are held on dry lake beds.

1937   The Southern California Timing Association (SCTA) is formed.

1948   The first major Sports Car Club of America (SCCA) race was held on the streets of Watkins Glen, New York.

1949   Wally Parks, SCTA president, becomes editor of *Hot Rod* magazine, and the National Hot Rod Association (NHRA) is formed.

1953   The first NHRA drag race is held in Pomona, California.

1960   Wood Brothers Racing discovers that they have an advantage over the competition by reducing the length of time during a pit stop.

1962   SCCA forms a professional racing class.

1962   Dave Elkins and Bill Robertson Jr. timed their trip from Tijuana, Mexico, to La Paz, Mexico, on a pair of Honda 250 motorcycles. Later that year, Chevrolet hires Bill Stroppe to build a fleet of trucks to do the same thing as a publicity stunt.

1967   Four teams of women participate in the 12 Hours of Sebring; the National Off-Road Racing Association (NORRA) holds the first Mexican 1000, which eventually became known as the Baja 1000.

1973   Mexican officials revoke NORRA's privileges to stage off-road races in Baja California, Mexico.

1975   SCORE International takes over organizing the Baja 1000, which becomes a loop race beginning and ending in Ensenada.

1979   Mexican officials restore the privilege of allowing the Baja 1000 to run from Ensenada to La Paz.

FURTHER READING

Burt, Bill. *Behind The Scenes of NASCAR Racing.* Osceola, Wisconsin: Motorbooks International, 1997.

Huff, Richard. *Behind The Wall: New Edition Captures Terry Labonte's 1996 NASCAR Season.* Chicago: Bonus Books, 1997.

Huff, Richard. *The Insider's Guide to Stock Car Racing.* Chicago: Bonus Books, 1997.

Olney, Ross R. *How to Understand Auto Racing.* New York: Lothrop, Lee & Shepard Books, 1979.

Waldron, Michael, ed. *John Force—I Saw Elvis at 1000 Feet.* Glendora, California: NHRA Specialty Publications, 1995.

ABOUT THE AUTHOR

Tara Baukus Mello is a freelance writer who specializes in the automotive industry. She has published over 1000 articles in newspapers and magazines. Baukus Mello is also the author of *Rusty Wallace*, part of the Race Car Legends series. A graduate of Harvard University, she lives in southern California, where she cruises the streets in her 1932 Ford pickup street rod with her husband, Jeff.

ACKNOWLEDGEMENTS

The author wishes to thank Jason Burdett, Bernie Fedderly, Rod Hall, Chad Hall, Todd Parrott, Tommy Mullis, and Dave Walsh for contributing to this book, and for sharing their love of racing with children throughout the country.

PHOTO CREDITS
Archive Photos, 10, 19, 24; Archive Photos/Authenticated, 2; A. F. P. from *Pictorial*, 39; AP LaserColor/Paul Velasco, 40; AP Laserphoto/Walt Weis, 34; AP Photo/*Inland Valley Daily Bulletin*, Chris Urso, 29; AP Photo/Alan Marler, 21, 30; AP Photo/*Richmond Times-Dispatch*, Stuart T. Wagner, 26; AP Photo/Kim Truett, 14; AP Photo/Tony Valainis, 22; AP/Wide World Photos, 48; Associated Press, AP, 32; Centerline Photography/ P. Hanson, 51; Centerline Photography/Kristian Pallesen, 53, 54, 57, 58; Daniel Joubert/Reuters, 46; "Paris Match" *Pictorial Parade*, 44; Photos courtesy of Indianapolis Motor Speedway © Indy 500 Photos, Indianapolis Motor Speedway Corp., 6, 11, 12, 16; Reuters, 36; Reuters/Tim Loyd/Archive Photos, 8.

INDEX